UNDERSTANDING THE THREE DIMENSIONS OF SIN

BY

BISHOP OCHEI INNOCENT

Contents

DEDICATION

TO THE HOLY SPIRIT OUR TEACHER.

CHAPTER ONE

HAVE YOU BEEN CROSS-CHECKING?

For some years, a young man had been looking for job. Despite all efforts, he could not get one. Eventually, he landed one as a Personal Assistant to a kind politician.

The politician loves to speak jaw breaking words.

The young man approached him and asked for a job description. In the same breathe, the young man asked what would do give offence to the employer.

The politician without hesitation said to him:

"You must avoid ***iberiberism.***"

The young man left.

Next day he assumed duty. He truly worked hard at it. Where he was expected to put in 8 hours, he put in 12. He wanted so much to please his employer that he over-labored himself.

After a while, he did a self assessment and scored himself excellent.

However, when it was time for the annual assessment and promotions, the politician scored him low.

Our friend was very sad and downcast. He went to the politician and asked what he did wrong.

The politician without hesitation said to him:

"You must avoid *iberiberism.*"

 The politician again without hesitation told him that though he was a hard worker his fault was that he exhibited *iberiberism.*

Our friend did not know the meaning of the word *iberiberism.* He also failed to ask the man for an explanation.

An associate advised him to see a wise man. He went. There, he complained that despite all his efforts, working extra time, the politician did not appreciate him. He lamented that instead the politician scored him zero.

The wise man asked when last he had a discussion with his employer. Our friend told him. The old man asked him whether he could remember the exact words the man used.

Our friend racked his brain and found the answer.

"Avoid ***iberiberism!***" he exclaimed.

"That is what he told me. Yes I remember now his exact words were: "avoid ***iberiberism***."

The old man considered the words for a while and he asked the young man what exactly is ***iberiberism***?

Of course our friend did not know.

The old white man frowned deeply as I asked:

"My friend, how can you serve or fulfill the aspirations of your employer when you do not understand what exactly he wants?"

He paused to look deeply at the person he was talking to.

"When he used the word ***iberiberism*** and you did not know the meaning, why did you not take pains to ask him or another person what he meant?"

The young man had no answer. Therefore, the wise man carried on:

"Some things should not just be assumed. You must take pains to identify what is needed. Once you do, you separate what has to be done promptly from similar things. That way, you can deliver exactly what is expected!"

Of course our friend thanked the wise man and went back to see his politician employer. Before then he had checked a dictionary in his attempt to find out what the word ***iberiberism*** means.

He could not find the meaning in any of the dictionaries he checked. That was because the word was derived from an

Igbo word pronounced "**iberib**e". This is a vast language group in eastern Nigeria.

The politician laughed. He said to the young man:

"If I really want to claim my right as your employer, I will ask you to refund all the monies you have received as salary so far. This is because you failed to do what I wanted.

"However, I will not do that. I expected you to ask me what exactly I meant by *iberiberism*. You are an American and I used a foreign word I picked up abroad. You did not know it and you did not ask questions. I took it that you were just desperate to land a job.

"When you were shortlisted for employment, three of you qualified and ranked neck-to-neck. It was difficult for me to select one out of the three of you.

"However you impressed me by asking what I wanted you to do as a personal assistant to me. And I replied that you should avoid ***iberiberism***. I expected you there and then to ask me for the meaning because I knew it was not an English word and since I derived it from Igbo language seeing that you were not Igbo, I would have explained it to you there and then but you failed to ask.

"I left you on the job because I knew that sooner than later you would realize that you had been foolish. The word ***iberiberism*** simply means an act of folly and it was foolish of you not to ask the meaning.

"As my PA, I wanted you to cross check all your facts and be wise in your answers to the media. Sometimes however, I found that you made press releases without cross-checking your facts, the very thing I feared.

"I did not sack you because I knew from experience that a day like this would come and you return to me.

"My own definition of a fool is a person who does not ask questions. A person who goes about taking actions based on assumptions. I hope you know that assumptions are subjective. Most times people think they know the right thing but they do not and unfortunately they know not that they know not. This has put many persons in trouble."

He further said to the employee:

"I can see that you are a Christian. In that case, you should know that Jesus Christ told his disciples that a blind man must not lead other blind men. Therefore, being the Personal Assistant to the leader that I am, your job is to make me have all the facts and figures to profess and not opinionate! That is what I hired you for.

"There is no way you can do this without asking questions. As a Christian myself, permit me to link what we are discussing to our Christian Faith. In all modesty, I tell you that there is no way you can be a good Christian without asking questions like the Berea Christians in the Bible who took pains to crosscheck everything they heard or were taught."

From that day the young man found and made it a duty to ask questions. He stopped taking everything or anything for granted. Even the ones he thought he knew, he cross-checked just in case he was wrong.

From that day also his job performance improved and he began to rank high in the esteem of his employer.

Now, to the important this important question:

CHAPTER TWO

WHAT HAS THIS GOT TO DO WITH OUR TOPIC?

Many of us Christians today take things for granted. Our Christianity and secular life are based on assumptions. Sorry to say this: we think we know but we know not.

It is so terrible that the Bible says:

Hosea 4:6
"My people are destroyed for lack of knowledge. Because you have rejected knowledge, I also will reject you from being priest for Me; because you have forgotten the law of your God, I also will forget your children.

We do not take pains to find out the meanings of words used in the scripture. Even the words that come to us from the altar in the day-to-day preaching.

Therefore, for us to effectively dissect the clause:

"The wages of sin is death."

We must apply the lessons learnt in the story of the young man above. People make mistakes for others to hear and learn. That is life.

We should avoid assumptions in our own life. We should humble ourselves and learn from others. No one man knows it all. That is what the young man's story has to do with our study.

CHAPTER THREE

WHAT REALLY IS SIN?

When the Bible uses some terms, we must realize that they are used on purpose. And in English language for instance, no two words mean exactly the same. That is why we must take pains to cross check. Let us give an example: Do not be silly and do not be stupid are similar but not exactly the same.

Therefore, we must make sure that we really understand what the Bible is saying or what the preacher wants us to understand. Otherwise, we go home with wrong perceptions and notions. I believe we have emphasized this point enough.

Let us take a close look at our key scripture:

Romans 6 verse 23;

[23] For the wages of sin is death, but the [a]gift of God is eternal life in Christ Jesus our Lord.

Our concern here is the first part of the verse. It says:

"The wages of sin is death."

It has everything to do with the topic of this book as we shall discover in the course of this discussion.

With the above in mind, and to help us comprehend better, I would like us to quickly look up the keywords in the said clause namely:

1. Wages.
2. Sin.
3. Death.

If we decode and demystify these words, we will discover that virtually all the problems of

mankind are summarized in these three simple looking words!

We must begin by asking ourselves **what exactly is sin**?

While this is not an academic lecture I believe it will be helpful for us to consult at least three dictionaries.

Cambridge English Dictionary defines sin as:

The <u>offence</u> of <u>breaking</u>, or the <u>breaking</u> of, a <u>religious</u> or <u>moral</u> <u>law</u>"

Collins Dictionary defines sin as:

"Sin or a sin is an <u>action</u> or type of <u>behaviour</u> which is <u>believed</u> to <u>break</u> the laws of God."

The Merriam Webster Dictionary on its part defines sin as:

1a : an offense against religious or moral law
b : an action that is or is felt to be highly reprehensible it's a sin to waste food
c : an often serious shortcoming : <u>fault</u>
2a : transgression of the law of God
b : a vitiated state of human nature in which the self is estranged from God"

Without prejudice to any of the above definitions, permit me to define sin simply as: **disobedience.** Sin is the breaking of the rules of engagement.

In every relationship there are ethical dimensions. In every relationship, there are expectations on the part all parties involved. You must have some conventional and non-conventional rules that bond the relationship. Some of them can be termed laws. Some of them are sometimes described as purely rules and regulations. They may be written, not written or both. It does not matter.

What matters is that those of us who are in such relationships understand that there are values to be recognized and sustained for there to be continuity of the relationship.

To further aid our study we need to realize that **relationship** simply means a bonding of two or more persons, things, events or beings both spiritually and physically for the purpose of getting along or depending on one another.

For more clarity, I took pains to ask the **Cambridge English Dictionary** its definition of relationship and this is what I got:

"The way in which two things are connected"

If we accept this definition, then we might as well note that **something** connects the two things. That something is what I choose to call: ***rules of engagement!***

When such rules are broken, there is sin. That is why when a son offends the father, we say**: "he has sinned against his father."**

Relationships as can be:

1. Between two or more humans. This includes but not limited to marriage, business partnerships, offices, associations, mentorships, friendships, enmity, lust, crime, etc.
2. Between man and spirits. Talking about spirits that includes God and demons.
3. The relationship can also be between handmade things and

man. For instance the porter and his pots.

4. Between man and animals. Such as between a horse trader and his wares.
5. Between man and institutions such as governments and schools.

All these have something that bonds them together. They may be called such different names as agreements, constitutions, bye-laws, rules and regulations, special and non special resolutions, ethics, family values, community ethos, divine laws, etc but they are one and the same. They play the singular role of helping the relationship live or thrive.

Permit me to elaborate on the example of such ethics guiding or facilitating relationships between handmade things and man and his pot. The potter might have the liberty to mould whatever he likes but there are rules to be obeyed. One of them is that he must carry the molded item with utmost care or it will fall. When the Potter's creation falls to the ground, it shatters! So to keep the relationship, he must keep the rule. To do otherwise would amount to sinning against the pot.

We must note and not very well that the relationship did not end because the molded item fell. No. The relationship ended because potter broke the law or rule or convention of caring for what it created by not carry the item with care.

 Permit me to also elaborate on man's relationship with animals. Take the poultry farmer. He has birds. The unspoken and perhaps unwritten agreement between him and the birds is that he will feed them for a time. From there, they give him eggs in return and perhaps even meat!

Every poultry farmer knows that there is that conventional law that he or she must play his part otherwise the relationship would end. When the Farmer fails to feed the birds, the birds naturally fail to lay eggs or yield meat up to the expectation of the farmer, if at all.

When the birds die for instance the relationship is broken. Such relationship did not break because the birds died. No. It broke because the Farmer did not obey the rules of farming birds.

In conclusion relationships are based on spoken and unspoken as well as written and unwritten rules and regulations. These are like the fuel that wc pour into our car. Without such fuel the vehicle might not move. In fact if you try to drive a car for long without putting oil in the engine, it will knock and that is probably the end of that car unless

another engine is purchased. Sin
destroys relationships.

CHAPTER FOUR

WHAT REALLY IS DEATH?

Now let us demystify the second keyword in our Bible verse. Remember that the verse says:

"The wages of sin is death."

We have taken a look at the word sin. Now let us look at death.

These also are how the dictionaries define the word "death".

Merriam Webster dictionary defines death as:

'A permanent cessation of all vital (see vital sense 2a) functions : the end of life'

This next definition is long. This is even a short except and it is from Encyclopedia Britannica:

"Many dictionaries define death as "the <u>extinction</u> or cessation of <u>life</u>" or as "ceasing to be." As life itself is notoriously difficult to define—and as everyone tends to think of things in terms of what is known—the problems in defining death are immediately apparent. The most useful definitions of life are those that <u>stress</u> function, whether at the level of <u>physiology</u>, of <u>molecular biology</u> and biochemistry, or of genetic potential. Death should be thought of as the irreversible loss of such functions."

For me I would simply say that death is **"cessation of relationship".** By this I understand that when a person or thing dies, it means that whatever relationship that existed with it ended. To me, when a man dies whatever relationship he has with animals, place and things, events, spirits, etc ceases!

I know you might have some questions at this stage but permit me to first illustrate this stand with your pets. You probably have a dog at home. You love this dog so much that you do not let it go hungry. Even when the dog does not ask, because of the love you have for the pet, you provide. Then suddenly this dog dies. There is nothing else to it than that that the relationship you had with the dog has ended.

You used to have him as a friend but now the dog is no more. It does not matter whether the remains of the dog were incinerated or buried in the ground. The most important thing is that the dog has ceased to exist and so too your relationship with the dog.

If you do not have a dog as pet you might have a car. You might also love your car so much or even your house. That love is a bonding factor that facilitated a relationship between you and the object of your admiration or submission.

It is not the purpose of this book to discuss the dimensions of relationship but permit me to mention that relationship could be in the form of:

1. Adoration
2. Submission
3. Partnerships
4. Friendship
5. Marriage
6. Consanguinity [Family]
7. Contiguity [Community]
8. Mentorship
9. Business.
10. Environmental,
11. Trade
12. Education
13. Events

14. Etc

These are things that create relationship.

Whatever the relationship is the truth remains that there is a bonding factor and it can be any of the above. Whatever precipitated that bonding subsists on values, principles, rules and regulations. When these rules and regulations are broken or disobeyed we say that we have sinned against each other and the relationship **ceases** or **dies:** which ever word you prefer.

You already know what I want to talk about: don't you? Remember that at the beginning of this book, we agreed that things are not always as simple as we think they are.

CHAPTER FIVE

WHAT THEN ARE WAGES?

Another word we might want to consider in that topic is **wages**! What do we exactly mean when we say wages?

Collins Dictionary defines wages as:

"Someone's wages are the amount of money that is regularly paid to them for the work that they do."

Dictionary.com defines wages as:

"Payment for services to a worker, usually remuneration..."

Again my own definition is:

Wages refer to the benefits, rewards, earnings, consequences and punishments of our actions,

labor, inputs, efforts or failure to labor, input or make any effort in whatever we do, expected to do or fail to do officially and unofficially regarding any relationship that we are into and that could be our relationship with God for instance.

Wages are what we earn for the things we do or fail to do. That includes sin! Taking the entire clause which says that *the wages of sin is death* we can conveniently, after looking at the various definitions above, submit that the rewards of disobedience in any relationship whatsoever is discontinuation or cessation or death of that relationship.

You may want to consider the relationship between a sick man and the oxygen machine. The sick man continues to survive because the oxygen is pumping in but the moment the machine is stopped the relationship ends and the man dies.

It should be there for crystal clear that

1. When we disobey the rules and conventions of any relationship there is a problem.

2. That problem eventually leads to the death of that relationship.

This brings us to a vital re-examination of relationships. There is a good reason for this.

CHAPTER SIX

THREE MAJOR DIMENSIONS OF MAN'S RELATIONSHIP AND HOW WE DESTROY THEM

Man's relationships can be subsumed under three major dimensions. The first is our relationship with God. From a Christian point of view we understand that there is a relationship between us and God. We are bonded with God by his mercies.

 This is how the Bible puts it:

Lamentations 3;22

"It is of the LORD'S mercies that we are not consumed, because his compassions fail not."

<u>1 Peter 1:3</u>

"Blessed be the God and Father of our Lord Jesus Christ! According to his great mercy, he has caused us to be born again to a living hope through the resurrection of Jesus Christ from the dead,"

This mercy is what enabled Him to create us in the first place and when we fell into sin out of the same mercy He sent his only begotten Son to die on the cross for you and me leading to our salvation and redemption.

John 3:16

"16 For God so loved the world that he gave his one and only Son, that

whoever believes in him shall not perish but have eternal life."

After our salvation and redemption the relationship continues as long as we recognize that God has expectations. Does he not have?

It is to His Glory that He is not a silent father. He boldly tells us via the scriptures that sin is a reproach and that the soul that sins shall die.

Ezekiel 18:20

20 The soul that sinneth, it shall die. The son shall not bear the iniquity of the father; neither shall the father bear the iniquity of the son: the righteousness of the righteous shall be upon him, and the wickedness of the wicked shall be upon him.

It follows therefore that those who know we have been redeemed must not continue in sin that Grace abide.

Romans 6:1
"What shall we say then? Shall we continue in sin, that grace may abound?"

When we continue in sin, we are with our own hands shattering the relationship that we have with God. The tragedy of sinning against God is that we die both to God and all its creations. The only place that can receive us is hell. More woefully we die to the spirit. We lose our eternal life.

Revelation 21:8

Revelation 21:8

8 But the cowardly, the unbelieving, the vile, the

murderers, the sexually immoral, those who practice magic arts, the idolaters and all liars—they will be consigned to the fiery lake of burning sulfur. This is the second death."

The second major dimension of man's relationships is the relationship we have with our fellow man. This comes in various ways and come in the following ways:

1. The relationship we have with our neighbors.
2. The relationship we have with our business partners.
3. The relationship we have with our immediate family. The relationship we have with our colleagues at work
4. Relationships with our school and class mates.

5. Relationship we have with our environments, Etc.

All these are governed by rules and regulations and we must find them and obey them. Failing to do so, leads to death of our relationship with these people and things. We are cut off.

I repeat for emphasis, when such rules are broken the relationship dies!

<u>When the Bible says that the wages of sin is death, what many of us fail to realize is that the Bible is not talking solely about spiritual applications</u>.

That scripture is also about daily living. Therefore this scripture applies also to our daily living. At this stage, can we ask some questions? I have asked some of mine already and you will find them in the next chapter .

CHAPTER SEVEN

WHY IS MAN SICK AT ALL?

 The third dimension of interest is how we relate with ourselves. To enable us understand this I want to ask the following questions:

Why do people go to prison?

Why do marriages crash?

Why do people fall sick?

Why are people poor? Why do governments fail?

Why do Nations go to war against one another?

Why do people give up easily and even in extreme cases commit suicide? Etc.

The answer to all these is that man continually sins against him. The Bible tells us that:

Jeremiah 17:9

"The heart is deceitful above all things, And desperately wicked; Who can know it?"

Man is innately wicked even unto himself. Jesus Christ describes the heart of man:

Matthew 13:15
"For this people's heart has grown callous; they hardly hear with their ears, and they have closed their eyes. Otherwise they might see with their eyes, hear with their ears, understand with their hearts, and turn, and I would heal them."

Man continues everyday to sin against himself by not resting. His body needs sleep, he is not kind to his own body enough to sleep knowing that his body needs the sleep to repair itself.

Man sees the laws of the land and deliberately goes out to break it mostly in his search for gold. As a result, he ends up in prison.

Man knows that in nine months time, if he is still alive, he will eat corn. He is so wicked that he would prefer to fold his arm and when the nine months comes, he begins to humiliate himself by begging for bread. He knows quite well that said that seed time and harvest time shall never cease but he does not listen.

He is so wicked that he does not forgive his self. The woman is from his flesh and God says whatever the offense forgive one another but man is so wicked to himself that he does not listen. So marriages break up.

Man is so wicked to himself that he does not remember that one day, he will leave this earth. Jesus Christ counsels him to stop laying up treasure on this earth where moth will eat it but in heaven but man is not listening. So he piles up gold at home and robbers come, kill him and take away the money.

God says that he that wields the sword shall die by the sword but man does not care. He only cares about temporary gains forgetting that the life of man is like the flowers that blossom in the morning and wither in the evening.

Man continues to make war on himself. Nations against nation when they know that a little dialogue could be better.

Man preys on young girls leaving them with unwanted pregnancies. This results in unwanted babies that end up not wanting anyone in return.

When will man take stock and end self abuse?

In a nutshell, he continues to abuse his body and still hopes for the best.

CHAPTER EIGHT

THE OPPOSITE OF SIN

If sin is disobedience, it follows that the opposite is **obedience**!

What does the Bible say about obedience?

The Bible is replete with verses on benefits of obedience. However the one that strikes me most says if we are obedient we shall eat the best of the Land. Is going to prison the best of the Land? The answer is no. Is being sick the best of the Land? The answer again is no. Is having our marriages break up, the best of the Land? No. Is being removed with shame as a ruler the best of the Land? The answer is no. Is not being able to feed your family the best of the Land? The answer is no.

If you are obedient you shall eat the best of the Land. That is the promise of God. Our relationship and ticket to the best of the land rests on obedience to God.

This is a promise predicated on something that you as a person have to do. You have to find out the written and unwritten laws of relationships and obey them in order to have the best of the Land.

Take marriage for instance. The Bible says submit to one another. Husbands love your wives like yourself. If we are obedient to these then there will be no problem. The relationship will be very sweet. The Bible says to all Christians including husbands and wives forgive one another. Pray for one another. Any marriage in which there is forgiveness can never crash.

All these are predicated on obedience. To disobey is sin and kills our relationship with our God, our self, our nation and environment as well as our fellow man.

Let us take governance as another example. This is what the Bible says. When the righteous is on the throne the people rejoice. What does it take to be righteous? With relation to governance it means being able to do the right thing that will bring joy to the people. This can only be done if you are right with your God. If you have fear of God you will rule as God wants it to be.

How does God want nations to be? He wants it to be like the example he showed us in the Garden of Eden a place where people will lack nothing in life. No one was put in bondage in Eden and there was no poverty.

This is only possible in a nation where there is no sin. For sin indeed is a reproach and it is that reproach that will

make the people to revolt and protest
and throw out their leaders.

Why do people go to prison? Being
incarcerated is not eating the best of the
Land. Rather it is a curse. People get to
jail because they have broken the laws of
the Land whereas God said to us in the
book of Romans chapter 13 that we
should obey those in authority over us. I
quote:

Romans 13:1-7

King James Version

*"Let every soul be subject unto the
higher powers. For there is no
power but of God: the powers that
be are ordained of God.*

*2 Whosoever therefore resisteth
the power, resisteth the ordinance
of God: and they that resist shall
receive to themselves damnation.*

3 For rulers are not a terror to good works, but to the evil. Wilt thou then not be afraid of the power? do that which is good, and thou shalt have praise of the same:

4 For he is the minister of God to thee for good. But if thou do that which is evil, be afraid; for he beareth not the sword in vain: for he is the minister of God, a tribute also: for they are God's ministers, attending continually upon this very thing.

7 Render therefore to all their dues: tribute to whom tribute is due; custom to whom custom; fear to whom fear; honour to whom honour."

Some have become sick because of their refusal to stop abusing themselves! Such people have indulged in excesses such as lack of rest. Some abuse drugs. Even some foods have to be taken in moderation and at appropriate time. Instead we abuse our body which is a form of disobedience.

These consequently lead to sickness. Some receive health warning signs but fail to go for medical attention. That in itself is a form of sin. The sin of negligence!. Sin indeed is disobedience of any kind.

 Many business partnerships have ended in disaster with some of them assassinating the other partner. Most of these are endangered because people fail to keep their promises or turn a partnership into a winner-takes-all. The laws or agreements that bond the partnership are discarded with impunity. All these are rooted in sin and the wages of sin is death. I am referring to unbelievers here who might not understand the Grace to forgive offenders.

For us Christians we must thank God for everything and not resort to self help. When man fails to give us what belongs to us and we let go in obedience to Christ, he is well able to pay exceedingly beyond our expectations!

Families crumble when there is disobedience. Children refuse to obey their parents but the Bible says honor thy father and thy mother that your days be long. Fathers also refuse to play their part by telling their children the truth as in the scriptures. Divine instructions by the almighty God of heaven and earth are disobeyed and you see families tearing apart.

 Job was a good man but he failed to instruct his children properly. Whenever they finish their partying Job will take an offering and try to cover up their sin but God cannot be mocked. When problem came, it came through the children first.

As parents we must strive to see that there is total obedience on our part to the scriptures by ensuring that the children are properly instructed. Doing otherwise is nothing but sin.

Deuteronomy 6:6 says that we should teach our children. The book of Proverbs also says train up a child as you would want the child to grow and when he grows up, he will not depart from it.

Many are in prison today because of covetousness. Their love for money exceeds their love for God. These persons are ready to do anything for money. They are not able to exercise restraint as God instructs us in the Bible. They substitute the love of God with the love for money. Some are so much after money that they can even go to the house of God and break into it without fear of consequences. Little wonder that jails in various nations are filled to the brim.

CHAPTER NINE

BENEFITS OF OBEDIENCE

I do not want to describe the benefits of obedience in my own words. Permit me therefore; **to bring to you seven scriptures** that wrap it all up and here they are below.

1. _Ephesians 6:1-3_

1 Children, obey your parents in the Lord, for this is right. 2 "Honor your father and mother"—which is the first commandment with a promise— 3 "so that it may go well with you and that you may enjoy long life on the earth."

<u>1.</u> *Luke 11:28*

28 *He replied, "Blessed rather are those who hear the word of God and obey it."*

<u>2.</u> *1 Peter 1:14*

14 *As obedient children, do not conform to the evil desires you had when you lived in ignorance*.

<u>1.</u> *Isaiah 1:19-20*

19 *If ye be willing and obedient, ye shall eat the good of the land:*

20 *But if ye refuse and rebel, ye shall be devoured with the sword: for the mouth of the* LORD *hath spoken it.*

5. DEUT.28:1-14

5. *28* **And it shall come to pass, if thou shalt hearken diligently unto the voice of the** LORD **thy God, to observe and to do all his commandments which I command thee this day, that the** LORD **thy God will set thee on high above all nations of the earth:**

2 **And all these blessings shall come on thee, and overtake thee, if thou shalt hearken unto the voice of the** LORD **thy God.**

3 **Blessed shalt thou be in the city, and blessed shalt thou be in the field.**

4 **Blessed shall be the fruit of thy body, and the fruit of thy ground, and the fruit of thy cattle, the increase of thy kine, and the flocks of thy sheep.**

5 *Blessed shall be thy basket and thy store.*

6 *Blessed shalt thou be when thou comest in, and blessed shalt thou be when thou goest out.*

7 *The* LORD *shall cause thine enemies that rise up against thee to be smitten before thy face: they shall come out against thee one way, and flee before the seven ways.*

8 *The* LORD *shall command the blessing upon thee in thy storehouses, and in all that thou settest thine hand unto; and he shall bless thee in the land which the* LORD *thy God giveth thee.*

9 *The* LORD *shall establish thee an holy people unto himself, as he hath sworn unto thee, if thou shalt keep the commandments of the* LORD *thy God, and walk in his ways.*

10 And all people of the earth shall see that thou art called by the name of the LORD; and they shall be afraid of thee.

11 And the LORD shall make thee plenteous in goods, in the fruit of thy body, and in the fruit of thy cattle, and in the fruit of thy ground, in the land which the LORD sware unto thy fathers to give thee.

12 The LORD shall open unto thee his good treasure, the heaven to give the rain unto thy land in his season, and to bless all the work of thine hand: and thou shalt lend unto many nations, and thou shalt not borrow.

13 And the LORD shall make thee the head, and not the tail; and thou shalt be above only, and thou shalt not be beneath; if that thou hearken unto the commandments of the LORD thy God, which I

command thee this day, to observe and to do them:

[14] And thou shalt not go aside from any of the words which I command thee this day, to the right hand, or to the left, to go after other gods to serve them.

    6. _John 8:51_

"Truly, truly, I say to you, if anyone keeps my word, he will never see death."

    7. _James 2:17_

So also faith by itself, if it does not have works, is dead.

I believe the above scriptures are self explanatory. I need add nothing to it.

Rather, I would like to end this little explanation by affirming that if we are obedient, we shall indeed eat the best of the land. For the words of God can never

be broken. God is not man that he
should ever lie nor repent of his words!

ABOUT THE AUTHOR

**BISHOP OCHEI INNNOCENT
IS THE PRESIDENT OF NEW**

DIMENSION SEMINARIES
INTERNATIONAL.

HE IS A MEMBER OF THE
INTERNATIONAL
FELLOWSHIP OF THE
CHRISTIAN CRISIS
CENTERS, USA.

HE IS MARRIED TO LIZZY
AND THEY ARE BLESSED
WITH FOUR GOD FEARING
CHILDREN.

THANKS ONCE MORE FOR READING THROUGH.

newochei@gmail.com

I ENCOURAGE YOU TO REACH ME WITH SUGGESTIONS YOU HAVE FOR THE IMPROVEMENT OF THIS BOOK IN THE NEXT EDITION.YOU CAN ALSO LEAVE AN HONEST REVIEW ON AMAZON.

ONCE MORE I THANK YOU FOR CHOOSING TO READ THIS BOOK AND I PRAY THAT ONE WORD REMAINS IN YOU LIFE FROM THIS LITTLE BOOK. -BISHOP OCHEI INNOCENT.

OTHER BOOKS BY THE SAME AUTHOR

1. HOW TO DEAL RUTHLESSLY WITH THE SPIRIT OF CONSPIRACY.

THE BOOK

THIS BOOK IS ABOUT THE DESTRUCTIVE POWER OF SIN. WHEN THE BIBLE SAYS THE

WAGES OF SIN IS DEATH, WHAT
EXACTLY DOES IT MEAN?

 THIS BOOK SEARCHES FOR THE
TRUE MEANING OF THIS
SCRIPTURE AND SHOWS THAT
ALL PROBLEMS OF MANKIND
ARE HINGED ON THIS SMALL
CLAUSE. ONLY A CRITICAL
EXAMINATION OF THE AFFAIRS
ON MEN IN THE LIGHT OF THIS
SCRIPTURES AND OTHERS,
WILL REVEAL THAT IF ONLY
MAN CAN REFRAIN FROM SIN,
ALL WILL BE WELL WITH OUR
PHYSICAL AND SPIRITUAL
LIVES.